29 WAYS TO INCREASE
—— YOUR ——
ROOM
RATES BY 200%

Michael J. Grimmé

About

AMC Liquidators

AMC Liquidators is one of the country's premier commercial and residential furniture liquidators – and the only one to specialize in both. AMC continually acquires fine furnishings and room décor from 4 & 5 star hotels, as well as excess inventories and closeouts of new fine furnishings from interior decorators and manufacturers. We offer these distinguished furnishings to the public and to businesses at reasonable prices. AMC purchases furniture from offices that are moving, renovating or closing. We also sell excess inventories of high-quality new furniture for home and office from the world's largest business-to-business services.

For more information, visit our website any time at: http://amcliquidators.com

To sign up for our newsletter and receive updated news and information, visit: http://amcliquidators.com/home/newsletter

Or – you can also call us directly, at: 888-840-6166

About

Michael J. Grimmé

The key to higher room rates is improving the guest experience. The better experience your guests have, the more your rooms are worth. When it comes to enhancing the guest experience, Mike Grimme is an expert.

Grimme opened his first boutique hotel in 1997, and sold it eight years later at four times its operating value. Over the course of the past two decades, as CEO and Founder of AMC Liquidators, Grimme has worked with a wide range of independent hotel properties, Assisted Living Facilities, and even Drug Rehab Centers. He has worked with them locally, nationally and internationally. From 1950s vintage properties to run-down motels, he has helped bring them back to life and converted them into high-value properties both quickly and cost-effectively. He has won a vast array of awards, including:

- The Fort Lauderdale Chamber of Commerce Small Business of the Year
- The South Florida Business Journal Small Business of the Year
- The Sun Sentinel Excaliber Award
- The Junior Achievement of South Florida Hall of Fame

Now...take a look at Grimmé's **29 Cost-Effective Ways to Increase Your Room Rates by 200%:**

THE LOBBY

1. Create a Space for Socialization

A hot trend driven by the millennial market segment is to create open lobbies conducive to socialization. Millennials are social beings. They like social spaces. Instead of hiding out in their room, they prefer to spend time in the lobby with their laptops or tablets. In order to design the lobby as a social space, it is important to include an area where guests can purchase drinks and snacks, as well as plenty of power outlets and a strong WIFI signal. However there is a caveat to this socialization suggestion: do not force people to sit next to someone they do not know. Avoid sofas and opt for single chair seating.

2. Choose Minimalist Lighting

Lighting in your lobby is absolutely crucial, even late at night. You never want a guest to walk into a dark reception area – it's a huge turn off. With that being said, however, you need to be cognizant of the lighting you choose. In general lighting should be minimalist. It should help to create a space that feels open and airy. By contacting a lighting consultant you can get the proper light for this space AND save money as lighting today is extremely energy efficient and prices continue to drop.

3. Opt for Consistent Styling

The styling of your lobby should always be consistent with the styling of the rooms. That means that if you are running a bed and breakfast in a refurbished Victorian home you don't want to create an ultra-modern lobby and then put antique four-poster beds in all of your rooms. It simply doesn't make sense and will disappoint your guests. If the styling of your rooms deviates substantially from the styling of your lobby your customer may feel duped once he gets his room key and opens up the door.

Consistency also needs to be maintained when it comes to maintenance. If your lobby has been redone in an ultra-modern style but your rooms look like something you might find in your grandmother's 1950s-esque home, again, your customer will feel duped. It is a wise idea to have a maintenance plan in place to coordinate consistent upgrades and improvements. Ultimately, consistency is crucial. Having a furniture restoration company come in on a regular basis to do in room touch ups and upholstery cleaning will stretch the life of your rooms and show the guest that you are fanatical about maintenance. This is a smart investment with a high ROI.

4. Choose Scents Wisely

Hotels often use scenting in order to mask any kind of unpleasant smells, such as mildew smells. This is especially common in beach areas where humidity levels tend to be high. While scenting is very often necessary, it is important not to over do it. If scents are over powering it is a huge turn off—customers will complain (and they may also wonder what kind of unpleasant odor you are working so hard to hide). Subtly is the trick to pulling off scenting. In general, you should choose either a linen scent or a lavender scent. These scents are pleasant yet subtle, and customers tend to associate them with cleanliness.

5. Use Personality Testing When Hiring Employees that Engage with Customers

It is important to hire wisely, especially when you are hiring the employees at reception. These are very often the first staff that guests will have contact with, so it is crucial to make a positive first impression. Your number one person should be your front desk person. They should be engaging, friendly, charismatic, and an adept problem solver. Remember, you can't teach personality.

It can be highly advantageous to personality profile every employee, particularly those who will be engaging with customers. Two reliable personality tests include the Predictive Index or the DISC Profile. There are actually Predictive Index and DISC test consultants that can come into your facility and develop a test shaped to your specific needs. These tests are incredibly easy and efficient, and can provide a tremendous amount of insight into potential employees. All in all, the goal is to make intelligent hiring choices. It usually runs about $200 for this test......very cheap compared to the cost of a bad hire or a bad first impression by a hotel guest.

6. Pay Attention to the Outdoors

It isn't just what is inside of your lobby; it is also what is outside of it. Your paint should be perfect, any landscaping or lawn should be perfectly maintained, and any signage should be in excellent condition. Walkways should always be kept clear of any snow, debris, leaves, or even mildew. You should also take care to properly light any kind of outdoor spaces, including walkways and landscaping. This is just as important as lobby lighting. After all, you don't ever want a customer to have to walk up to your establishment in the dark. Not only is this unwelcoming, it is also a huge (and potentially expensive) safety hazard.

If you plan to place any kind of furniture in outside spaces, be sure to do your research before making a purchase. Always go with furniture that has a track record of success in outdoor environments. Keep in mind that there is a huge difference between porch furniture and furniture designed to handle exterior elements, including sunlight, rain, snow, etc. Salt air is particularly BRUTAL to outdoor furniture. Make appropriate choices.

THE ROOM

7. Opt for High-Quality Used Furniture over Low-Quality New Furniture

Avoid any kind of low-quality furniture, especially Formica case goods. While these are typically low-priced, they are essentially made out of pressed board (often cardboard). It will be obvious to the guest that the furnishings are cheap, which signals you aren't truly invested in their experience. With any kind of humidity or even a damp towel, the surfaces will quickly bubble up and delaminate. This is impossible to repair cost effectively. Furthermore, cheap furniture has virtually no resale value, so it is a very poor investment.

If you can't afford new high-quality furniture, opt for quality pre-owned furniture from the top hotels. Target furniture coming from 4 and 5 star hotels. High end hotels typically have superior quality, well built, durable high end furniture in their rooms, not cheap pressed board furniture, maintain it well, and renovate every 5 to 7 years. The soft furnishings are often replaced on a shorter cycle. Top hotels have very strict furniture standards, and in many cases they have over a century worth of experience purchasing furniture. Any five-star hotel will do a considerable amount of research when furnishing a room, and will often spend up to forty thousand dollars per a room. The bottom line is that they are looking for furnishings that will last. The average hotel nightstand, for example, can hold up to 350 pounds. Buying pre-owned is a lucrative option. You can purchase high-quality furniture that is only a few years old at a small fraction of what these hotels paid, that can be used for 10 to 15 more years.

All in all, purchasing quality pre-owned furniture from high end is a wise choice, and it will likely last you for many years to come. If you are on a budget it is a much, much better option than buying furniture from a cheap case good manufacturer or an inexpensive retailer. When making pre-owned furniture purchases it is always ideal to purchase directly from a experienced liquidators handling these projects. Experienced liquidators handle these projects because they have the know how, equipment and warehousing to move at the pace needed by these hotels. Hotel conversion situations where a hotel is converting from a hotel to a condo, for example, can present an excellent purchasing opportunity. Before purchasing you will want to examine the inventory in their warehouse in order to ascertain quality and condition.

8. Ditch the Vertical Blinds

When it comes to choosing window treatments, vertical blinds are often a common option. However, they are an incredibly flawed option. Vertical blinds get dirty very easily, making it difficult to maintain a clean, sleek appearance. Furthermore, they can prove to be quite noisy if the windows are left open, and also fail to provide adequate light blockage. Drapes with black out shades are a far better option and are typically available through hotel liquidators at a great price. Look for a liquidator that can alter them in house to your size requirements.

9. Repaint Rooms a Basic Colo

When in doubt, always opt for off-white rooms. This creates a clean, modern feel. A bit of color never hurts, however if you decide to add a bit of color choose wisely. Pastel colors like pink of green are all passé, and they will date your facility. Similarly, any kind of mauve color is never a good choice, as it is dark and depressing. Remember, the goal is create a vibe that is clean and modern.

10. Never Let the Customer See the Bedframe

A customer should never, ever, see the bedframe. If possible, it is advisable to get rid of bedframes all together by using box bedframes that sit on the floor. This keeps the space underneath the bed totally enclosed, eliminating a number of common problems. First and foremost, this alleviates pressure on housekeeping to keep the space under the bed pristine. There is no need to worry about labor-intensive under the bed vacuuming or dusting. Secondly, it also helps to mitigate the problem of lost items. A customer cannot say, "I lost my diamond watch underneath the bed," or "My glasses fell off my nightstand and rolled under the bed," as there literally is no space under the bed.

If, for whatever reason, box bedframes are not a feasible possibility be sure to invest in high-quality dust ruffles. You will also need to make sure that your cleaning staff keeps the space underneath the beds absolutely spotless, totally free of any debris or dust. Remember, customers will always take a peek underneath the bed to ascertain the cleanliness of your rooms.

11. Invest in High-Quality Mattresses

You want your guests to love your mattresses. Ideally, customers should love your mattress so much that they want to take it home with them when they leave. That means you need to make intelligent choices when mattress shopping. Ideally, you will want to choose something with a coil count above 800. Just like with furniture, if you can't afford high quality new mattresses opt for something used. Many four- or five-star hotels replace their mattresses on a frequent cycle, often 5 years, and you can buy pre-owned mattresses from hotel furniture liquidators at very attractive prices. Keep in mind that high-quality mattresses have a much longer lifespan, and can often last up to a decade. Therefore, a high-quality mattress is well worth the investment.

12. Upgrade the Lighting

Mounted lighting is a thing of the past. It is outdated, and automatically makes a room seem passé. Update to something more modern. And when buying lamps, keep in mind that you can never have too many lamps in a room.

13. Lower the Artwork

Artwork is most often hung by men, which means that it often perceived by women to be too high. When art is too high it is awkward and uncomfortable. Lowering the artwork is a simple tweak that can significantly enhance the aesthetic appeal of your rooms.

14. Add More Power Outlets

You can never have too many power outlets in a room. You never want to force a customer to un-plug something necessary (such as a television or a light) in order to be able to charge a phone, iPad or laptop. Try to make sure to always leave one open plug on each outlet. That means that if you have a lamp desk plugged into an outlet there should also be a free plug for your customer to use. Try buying lamps from hotel furniture liquidators that have power outlets in their bases.

15. Ditch the Bedspreads and Invest in Sashes

Bedspreads are a thing of the past. Customers want to know that everything on a bed has been washed before they climb into it, and they are often skeptical that bedspreads have been washed. People automatically assume that bedspreads harbor bed bugs and they are also difficult to clean, which drives up operational costs. Instead of bedspreads, it is advisable to use sashes. These run along the end of the bed, helping the bed to stay clean when people put their feet up. Sashes are low maintenance, aesthetically pleasing, and easy to clean.

16. Purchase Linens that Can be Bleached

Pillows, linens, blankets—anything that you put in the wash needs to be bleached in order to kill any potential bed bugs. That means that you can't purchase anything that would be harmed or damaged by bleach.

17. Clean Your Upholstered Furniture

There is no excuse for dirty upholstery. Do your research before purchasing upholstered goods. Choose upholstery that is easy to clean and low maintenance. This is especially true in beach areas, where sunscreens and tanning oils are likely to come into contact with your upholstery. These kinds of substances can easily stain upholstery, and if you haven't chosen a material that is easy to clean, you then run the risk of having to replace furniture each time a child comes in from the beach covered in sunscreen and takes a seat on the couch. Never assume that customers won't notice upholstery stains—they absolutely will. If something is stained you need to get rid of it. Remember the state of your furniture speaks volumes. Well-maintained, stain-free furniture shows that your facility is attentive to details, it shows you care about the quality of your customer's experience.

18. Toss the Silk Plants

Do not, under any circumstances, put silk plants in your rooms. Not only are they outdated they are also major dirt catchers. If you want to have decorative pieces in the room, find items that are easy to keep clean and do not collect dust. Bear in mind that these decorative pieces often "grow legs" and disappear. Lock them down or prepare for the worst.

19. Make Eco-friendly Adjustments

In today's world, guests are eco-conscious, especially millennials. They want to stay at properties that have made a proven commitment to the environment. Your waste baskets ideally should have a separate area for recyclables. From soy based bedding to recycled furniture whenever and wherever you can make an eco-friendly adjustment, do so....and tell your customers you are doing it!

20. Add Decorative Mirrors

You must have a dressing mirror in each room. If you are Triple A rated you must have a five foot mirror in each room. In addition to this mirror, it is highly advisable to have a second, decorative mirror. This will open up the room, making it brighter and creating the illusion of more space.

21. Add an Information Packet to Each Room

Add a small binder to each room that contains valuable local information, including places to see, a list of recommended restaurants, emergency facilities, etc. Make sure all information in this binder is always accurate and current. Although customers can go online and find this info, it is still a nice amenity for them.

THE BATHROOM

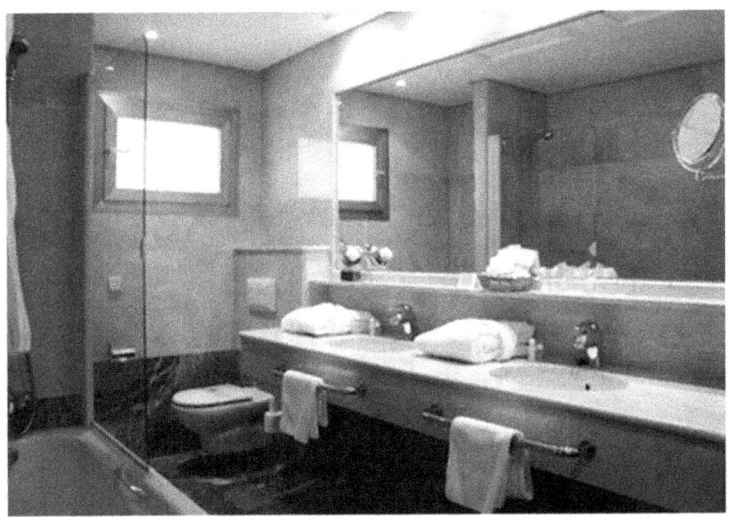

22. Pay Attention to the Top of the Shower

In general, you absolutely need to fanatical about bathroom cleanliness. No evidence of previous guests should be left anywhere in the room, especially the bathroom. Always instruct your housecleaning staff to keep the top of the shower clean. It is often out of sight, and therefore forgotten. However, guests will also inevitably run their hands on the top of the bed headboard and along the top of the shower curtain rod to judge the cleanliness of your facility. Cleanliness boosts value.

23. Fix Anything that is Broken

Every single bathroom in your facility should be in absolute perfect operating condition. The toilets need to run perfectly, the sink shouldn't leak a drop, and the bathtub stopper should function flawlessly. If something breaks, fix it or replace it immediately. Anything that isn't working properly, especially in the bathroom, will detract value from your rooms.

24. Hire a Grout Cleaning Service

You absolutely must keep the grout in your bathrooms clean. It is one of the first things that customers notice when they walk into a bathroom. It is good to have a grout cleaning service come in on a regular basis to freshen up the grout. This service isn't too expensive, and it can significantly enhance the appearance of your bathroom.

THE WEB

25. Highlight Your Strengths

In order to effectively market yourself, you need to understand your facility's strengths and play them up on your website. If you offer free WIFI, say so. If you have an award-winning luxury spa, include photos.

26. Include Photos & Videos on Your Website

Always include photos and video of your lobby, rooms, restaurant, pool area, spa, and other common areas etc. on your website. 360-degree photos and video should also be added if possible. Drone video has become so cheap that this is also an interesting option. Most hotels have several different room types and all types should be photographed. Photographing the view from the rooms is also a nice touch.

27. Actively Monitor Social Media Sites & Hotel Review Sites

In today's world, social media is absolutely crucial. You should be actively cultivating a presence on all major social media sites, such as Facebook, Twitter, Instagram, etc. Not only should you actively be posting content to these sites, you should also be reviewing what your customers say on your social media accounts. This can provide you with valuable insight into guest experience, helping you to better understand your strengths and make tweaks to any issues that many guests have complained about. You should also be regularly reviewing reviews posted on hotel review sites, such as Travelocity.

28. Always Address a Bad Review

There is no denying it—a bad review can hurt. While it is never pleasant to read nasty words about your business, it is crucial to put your feelings aside and address the review. Every hotel has their issues from time to time. The key is to act on the issues promptly in a positive way and post how you handled the issue. This will go a long way to bolster your reputation in a positive way.

29. Solicit VIP Testimonials

If any celebrity or high-level businessman stays at your facility, always ask for a testimonial. If you can, get photos of these individuals at your facility. Putting these testimonials and photos on your website will always raise your profile in a positive way.

I hope these tips prove useful. Good luck!